# A TEACHER'S RESOURCE BOOK FOR *MAY 4TH VOICES: KENT STATE, 1970*

## A PLAY BY DAVID HASSLER

*Teaching History and Social Justice in the Classroom*

*Edited by John L. Morris, Ph.D.*

*with contributions by educators from*
*around the United States*

A COPUBLICATION OF THE KENT HISTORICAL SOCIETY AND

THE KENT STATE UNIVERSITY PRESS

KENT, OHIO

# CONTRIBUTORS

Grateful thanks to the following educators for their contributions to this resource book:

Judith Atkins, Teacher of Art, Theodore Roosevelt High School, Kent, Ohio

Doris Baizley, Founding Member, LA Theaterworks, Los Angeles, California

Katherine Burke, Instructor, School of Theater and Dance, Kent State University, Kent, Ohio

Patrick Chura, Ph.D., Associate Professor of English, University of Akron, Akron, Ohio

Christina Dreher-Rodesheim, Teacher of History, Theodore Roosevelt High School, Kent, Ohio

Margana Fahey, Teacher of English, Theodore Roosevelt High School, Kent, Ohio

Richard M. Foote, Vice President, Business Development and Client Services, The Davey Tree Expert Company, Kent, Ohio

Cara Gilgenbach, Head, Kent State University Libraries Special Collections and Archives

David Hassler, Author, *May 4th Voices: Kent State, 1970*

Julie Healy, Teacher of Physical Education, Theodore Roosevelt High School, Kent, Ohio

Nikki Marchmon-Boykin, Teacher of History, Theodore Roosevelt High School, Kent, Ohio

David Massucci, Teacher of English, Theodore Roosevelt High School, Kent, Ohio

John L. Morris, Ph.D., English Instructor, Shaker Heights, Ohio

Noël Palomo-Lovinski, MFA, Associate Professor, School of Fashion Design and Merchandising, Kent State University, Kent, Ohio

Stephen Paschen, Archivist, Kent State University, Kent, Ohio

Major Ragain, Poet and Lecturer, Kent, Ohio

Heidi Summerlin, Graduate Student in History, Youngstown State University, Youngstown, Ohio

H. Anderson Turner III, MFA, Director of Galleries, School of Art, Kent State University, Kent, Ohio

Ohio Arts Council
A STATE AGENCY
THAT SUPPORTS PUBLIC
PROGRAMS IN THE ARTS

© 2013 by The Kent State University Press
All rights reserved
ISBN 978-1-60635-166-6
Manufactured in the United States of America

All photographs not otherwise credited are courtesy of Kent State University Libraries' Special Collections and Archives May 4th Collection.

The poem "May 4, 1970/A Memory" by Maj Ragain was first published in 2005 by Pavement Saw Press, Columbus, Ohio, in *Hungry Ghost Surrenders His Tacklebox* by Maj Ragain and is reprinted with permission.

Cataloging information for this title is available at the Library of Congress.

17  16  15  14  13      5  4  3  2  1

# CONTENTS

# INTRODUCTION

*John L. Morris, Ph.D., English Instructor, Shaker Heights High School*

One of the most compelling aspects of visiting the Vietnam Veterans Memorial Wall in Washington, D.C., is how the black granite begins at a subtle point and, before you realize it, overwhelms you with the magnitude of its dark mass and the names of fallen soldiers etched on its reflective black exterior. What Maya Lin designed in honoring Vietnam Veterans is overpowering and undeniable. The Wall is a perfect metaphor for the enormity of the Vietnam War, how it began unobtrusively and overwhelmed the United States emotionally, psychologically, and politically.

The Wall also expresses what many feel when considering the events surrounding the war, including May 4th, 1970, and the shootings that took place at Kent State University. The Kent State Shootings, like the Wall, also seem impenetrable and opaque. The Vietnam War and the events at Kent State appear larger than life and difficult to navigate. The loss of those four lives indelibly marked our collective conscious concerning what it is to be a member of our democratic society and how we function in the face of conflict and tragedy.

What David Hassler has created through *May 4th Voices* is a window into the events of this tumultuous era. It is another type of memorial to the Vietnam War and those that lost their lives. However, in this instance, the lives lost were not of soldiers, but of innocent students protesting the actions of their government. Through the real voices of townspeople, students, National Guardsmen, protestors and professors, we experience this devastating moment in American History and the Vietnam War Protest Movement. With poet Maj Ragain as our guide, we witness the events leading up to, including and leading away from the May 4th Shootings as never before, through the voices of those who were actually there. In contrast to the hard granite of the Vietnam War Memorial we are offered the soft humanity of the voices of participants in the tragic circumstances of the May 4th shootings.

Another powerful element of the Vietnam Veterans Memorial Wall is that as you read the names on the Wall, it becomes difficult because you see yourself and the images of others reflected on the Wall's mirror-like surface. Here, again, *May 4th Voices* resonates with its antecedent in Washington. As the reader listens to the voices of these protestors, family members, teachers and students, it is impossible not to hear one's own voice and the voices of those you know in these words from the past. There is humor, love, spiritual longing, indecision, passion, fear and the full spectrum of human emotions expressed in these words. Just like the photographer attempting to capture an image of a name on the wall, it is impossible to read *May 4th Voices* and not see a reflection of yourself.

As someone who has had the privilege of teaching this text and seeing this play performed, I have been transformed by the experience. What makes this study guide an extension of this experience is the opportunity it allows teachers and students to dig even further into May 4th 1970 through the Kent State Shooting Oral History Project and access to the primary documents and interviews that David Hassler utilized to shape *May 4th Voices*. The primary source of the online archive, including an easy finder's guide, offers full transcripts for all the interviews and audio for nearly 90 percent of them. This unique resource offers teachers the opportunity to create lessons designed to guide students through this digital archive. The potential here for students to explore this important moment in 20th century American History through first person narrative, American Government, Theatre, Literature, Social Justice, Music, Art and related subjects is limited only by a teacher's imagination. We have begun this exploration in the scene-by-scene study guide in the pages that follow.

I have the same emotional and intellectual response to *May 4th Voices* as I have to visiting the Vietnam Veterans Memorial Wall. After both experiences, I know that what I have witnessed makes me want to change myself, my country and the way I relate to the world. That is what a memorial can do.

It creates a space and time for deep reflection. The difference between the Vietnam Veterans' Memorial in D.C. and the memorial contained within *May 4th Voices* is that these emotions evolve and take shape whenever I read the text. I hope this play and study guide can do the same for you and your students.

# MAY 4, 1970/A MEMORY

*Maj Ragain*

Photo by Mathias Peralta.

*Excerpts from Maj Ragain's prose poem form the Narrator's voice in the play* May 4th Voices, *by David Hassler. The entire poem is reproduced here.*

I first came to Kent on a July morning, 1969, having driven all night from Illinois, hungover, raw, leaving behind the carnival undertow of my youth, hot dreams and crazy love. I first saw the town from Route 59, Stow, the cluster of buildings catching the sun. I remember thinking it looked like the photographs of an Italian town reared up in the sky. Years later, when I got to Italy, some of the towns looked, from a distance, like Kent. I was glad to find a river and railroad tracks, a brick train station, water and steel joining this to that. Haymaker Parkway was still on the drawing boards. I entered Kent over the old Main Street bridge and right onto Water Street. Always find a Water Street. Within a block or two, I came across a young man in a rocking chair, sitting in front of a store, orange and white facade, big letters THE SECOND STORE. His long brown hair hung nearly to the ground off the back of the rocker. He wore an olive drab fatigue jacket and was reading a *Ramparts* magazine up close, his rimless glasses on the tip of his nose. I'll start here, I thought, and introduced myself. The first citizen of Kent to whom I spoke was Mort Krahling. One of the spiritual voices of the place, whose spare and beautiful poems sing the soul of Kent, its mysteries, pointing to that which cannot be seen. He was a man whom Thoreau had in mind when he wrote of poets as the means by which a place comes to contemplate its own nature. I was to know Mort for thirty years till his death in December of 1998. The place came forth to meet me in the guise of Mort.

I was twenty nine years old. I settled into the Allerton apartments at eighty bucks a month and began life as a graduate student. I wasn't much good at it, spent too much time at Walter's Bar on Water Street, gave my heart away every full moon and took incompletes in my classes. Spring, 1970. Nixon had escalated the Vietnam War with the bombing of Cambodia. There was anger and disappointment. By then, the Vietnam Veterans Against The War had organized in Kent. I remember them stopping the traffic on Main street, in front of the Brady Cafe, a

4

hundred or more of them, marching rag tag, bearded, silent, some amputees, a couple of men rolling wheelchairs, Coxie's army come home. Later that day, the vets held a teach-in at Fred Fuller park, under the big trees, a small encampment of listeners bending to the hard lessons.

Friday, May 1, 1970. I was downtown in Walter's Bar, drinking Rolling Rock and riding a warm spring Ohio night. Around eleven o'clock, after an NBA finals game on TV, the bars swelled over into the street, blocking traffic.

Someone dumped a trash container and lit a bonfire on the centerline, then another. The Chosen Few, a biker gang from Youngstown, rumbled in. The crowd parted to let them through. They did wheelies back and forth on Water Street. I remember the biker they called Pappy—the name in bold yellow on the back of his colors jacket—brown beard, tied back ponytail, a skinny yokum guy who looked older than his years. Pappy took off his floppy hat, sat cross-legged in the middle of the street. As the bikers wheelied by, the riders slam-dunked beer bottles into Pappy's hat. At every dunk—nobody missed—the crowd cheered. I cheered. Blake had it right. *Exuberance is beauty. Energy is eternal delight.* The horses of instruction were in the barn. The tigers of wrath were teaching us their wisdom. It was crazy springtime in a country still young, blood surge, hot youth, a protest against every tight bunghole, against every official hand turning the screws on freedom. It was *one, two, three, four, we don't want your fucking war,* just like they told you. Only louder. And everybody meant it. We were together in an odd, unmistakable brotherhood/sisterhood I have not felt since, as if we'd all been swallowed by the same whale. The state troopers stormed in with white helmets/plexiglass masks and billyclubs. Mort Krahling and I ducked into his junkstore across the street from Walter's. That building is gone now. Mort is gone.

Monday, May 4. A clear, warm spring day, everything in blossom. I woke to an apartment full of people. Maureen Halpin and three friends from Edwardsville, Illinois, had stopped overnight on their way to the Bobby Seale/Black Panther trial on the east coast. I drove up to Satterfield Hall. Classes had been canceled. A noon rally had been called on the Commons. I began walking toward the Commons with my friends, Steve Newmann and Jim Hayes, a veteran, when we saw the first white plumes of tear gas and heard the barking of a National Guard officer over a bull horn, demanding that the crowd disperse. I knew I couldn't crutch walk away from the tear gas and retreated to Satterfield. It must have been just after noon when I watched a squad of National Guardsmen kneel, lock, and load in front of Satterfield. It never occurred to me, nor to anyone else I talked to, that the Guard carried live, steel jacketed ammunition. We did not think of ourselves as the enemy, dissidents but not enemy, believing the Guard to be on a peacekeeping mission, a civil action against an unarmed citizenry. Jeff Miller, who was a student of my friend Mike Danko, was shot in the mouth at a distance of several hundred yards. That night I sat with Mike out in his yard, in the rain, as he drank and wept. I drank with him but couldn't find tears. I held him. He would not be consoled. As far as I know, Mike still isn't consoled. Something broke off inside him, like one of those city block sized chunks that shivers loose from an Antarctic ice cap and begins to wander the cold seas. Something in Mike broke away and drifts inside him to this day.

I offer not a consolation but an understanding. I know they are not the same. The Buddhists tell us we all have three hearts, linked one to the other, like Christmas lights in a series. First is the heart of compassion, then the heart of love, finally the heart of wisdom. They open in that order and no other. Compassion, that heart once opened, prompts the opening of the heart of love and that in turn signals the opening of the heart of wisdom. Meet your rage on the threshing floor of the first heart. No other way. No love, no wisdom, without compassion. That simple. Compassion, from its Greek root, means feeling the viscera of the other. Feeling the spleen, the heart, the guts of the other. The other is whoever is not you. Feel that. Start there. The viscera of the students. The viscera of the Guard.

Beyond that conviction, I am lost. At sunset May 4, I left Kent, headed back to Illinois. The National Guard had sealed off the town. I drove up to one of the checkpoints, barricades, across Route 43, just south of the 261 intersection. A young, ill at ease Guardsman checked my driver's license, took down the information on a clipboard and set aside the barricade. As my wife, Kathy, and I drove through, and I was a shaggy, bearded fella back then, the National Guard officer, a lieutenant, gave us the finger, smacking his elbow in his cupped hand for emphasis. I am his other. He is mine. If there is to be peace, he must feel my viscera. I must feel his. I don't know another way.

Thirty years later, spring comes again. I live on the other side of the Cuyahoga River in a small house on a dead end street. I haven't gotten very far. This afternoon, my daughter cut the grass. I weeded the flower bed. Maintenance. Provisional orders. A wooden fence marks where our property ends and the neighbor's begins. Everything is in its place. When I look up, it is all vast emptiness. We name the planets after gods we have never seen. We imagine heaven out there.

On the bookshelf in the living room is a Christmas gift from my daughter, a photo of the two of us, her arms round my neck. Meg is beaming. I am baring my teeth neath my mustache. I have always been happier than I look, happier than you think I am. At the top of the photo, Meg has printed, in her small hand, *What is not love is fear.* She said she found it in a book, in a doctor's office. I have puzzled over these words everyday. *What is not love is fear.* Something in me resists this stark, unequivocal proposition, distrusts it as neat sophistry, the kind of glibness which always rankles me. But, these words are Meg's gift to me. She has come a long way to tell me this. What it asks of me seems beyond doing. If it is true, then I have lived much of my life in vague, dull fear, acting out of that.

Today, I receive a letter from Adam Brodsky, along with his poems for the annual *Jawbone* book. At the close, Adam has included a few lines from the *Rig Veda*, the ancient Hindu text.

*Two birds, inseparable companions, are perched on the same tree: one eats the sweet fruit; the other looks on without eating.*

One bird, whose name is love, eats the sweet fruit; the other, whose name is fear, looks on without eating. Love and fear are inseparable in this life, as are the self and the other. Each is a witness to the other. *What is not love is fear.* They are inseparable companions. We must meet them on the threshing floor of the heart. Each must come to know the other.

Tomorrow, I'll find my way up to the Commons to hear the ringing of the bell to commemorate the dead and the wounded. The bell is a voice. Everything in Kent is in blossom. Every blossom is listening.

# MAY 4TH VOICES:
## THE HISTORICAL ARTIFACT AS LITERARY TEXT

*Patrick Chura, Ph.D., Associate Professor of English, University of Akron*

*Patrick Chura has had extensive experience using* May 4th Voices *by David Hassler with his students. In this article, he reflects on that experience and discusses what he has learned. Personal responses to the work, drafted by his students, follow his remarks.*

May 4th Voices was the key factor in my decision three years ago to develop a university course on literature of the Vietnam War and to include a substantial unit on the Kent State tragedy. After attending the play's premier in May 2010, I contacted David Hassler and asked to use the play as a reading in my senior-level literature seminar at the University of Akron. David responded generously, first by providing me with an actors' copy of the script and a DVD of the filmed premier, then by having lunch with me to talk about how the play was written, and finally by visiting the new seminar during the first semester it was taught.

David began his visit by having the class take turns reading aloud from the play. We were fully involved with the text and unexpectedly stirred by the experience of adopting its voices as our own. Listening to the undergraduates articulate the reactions and political stances of protesters, teachers, guardsmen, and Kent residents young and old helped bridge a more-than-forty-year historical gap, preparing the twenty-something students for a very engaged discussion of the Vietnam era political atmosphere in Northeast Ohio and nationwide. Afterward, David shared his own memories of Kent in 1970 and described his play's purpose as "opening up a conversation we've never fully had" about the "living wound" of May 4.

Before we could move into our usual treatment of the work as a literary text, however, the students asked our guest some sophisticated questions: How had the play's voices been selected and arranged? Was the oral history in *May 4th Voices* transcribed verbatim? How extensively did he as scripter ma-nipulate oral history passages in order to achieve narrative or emotive effects? How did he decide which voices to include? Obviously, the students were seeking ways to classify the play and its elements in relation to other works on the syllabus and to learn something about how Hassler's work was able to move readers and audiences. They took this approach, I think, because they realized the play was unique in form. We had already studied fiction, poetry, nonfiction, film and music about the Vietnam War, but *May 4th Voices* was different, not simply because it was a staged drama, but because the raw material out of which it was created—oral histories—lent it an unusual kind of authenticity.

Over several discussions immediately following David's visit, we decided that *May 4th Voices* constitutes a particularly good example of verbatim theatre—a relatively new form of documentary drama in which plays are constructed from the precise words spoken by people interviewed about a particular event or topic. Other high profile verbatim theatre pieces include *Twilight: Los Angeles 1992,* a play about the LA riots following the disposition of the Rodney King case, and *The Laramie Project* by Moises Kaufman, about the hate-murder of Matthew Shepard in Wyoming in 1998. Like *May 4th Voices,* these works achieve realism and emotional impact not from elaborate sets, props, or stage effects, but from the audience's awareness that the words of the scripted text are those of real people rather than fictional characters. In verbatim theatre, persons with special connections to the play's subject are given the freedom to recount—without mediation—their diverse and conflicting but often eloquent stories. Verbatim theatre involves us on an immediate, human level in a type of history-making that takes place in reality, among ordinary members of communities.

The implicit reminders contained in Hassler's play—that we must speak and that we are all in some sense responsible for history-making—seem especially necessary today. The long-term response to the Kent State tragedy displays classic symptoms of repressed, throttled communication. As Judith Herman observed in *Trauma and Recovery,* "The ordinary response to atrocities is to banish them from consciousness." *May 4th Voices* is redemptive and cathartic because it exposes communal anxieties and silences, creating a conversation in which all voices can be heard and all points of view included without engendering fear, hatred or anger. Bringing *May 4th Voices* into the classrooms of Northeast Ohio has already begun the process of moving beyond silencing polarization, pointing instead toward viewing conflict as an opportunity to create empathy and positive change.

But the efficacy of *May 4th Voices* is certainly not limited to Ohio. The play enables all teachers of literature and culture studies to pose broad and valuable questions about the relationship between historical and literary truth. After discussing the play as verbatim theatre, I had the students read a chapter from Hayden White's *Tropics of Discourse* entitled "The Historical Text as Literary Artifact." White, a historian and literary critic, observes that we who work with literature in the classroom have tended to presuppose "a radical opposition" between history and fiction, between facts and the imagination. White reminds us that historical narratives are best thought of as "invented verbal forms," and that the historian is above all a storyteller. "Emplotment" is the process of fashioning stories out of facts or chronicles, and when history is emplotted or shaped into narrative, it ceases to be history altogether and becomes a hybrid genre. It may sound counterintuitive, but histories gain power through their success in making stories out of "mere facts." For White, the problem with this process is that most histories necessarily indoctrinate their audiences by informing them what to take from events.

In *May 4th Voices,* however, Hassler as historian resists the impulse to explain, instead putting faith in a collection of story fragments and testimonies contained in an archive. He works not through deduction but inductively, merely collecting external verbal artifacts—the "voices" contained in by the Kent State Oral History Project. It is important that the voices largely remain artifacts, only lightly edited by a "scripter" intent on preserving them, and

that they become a literary text only by being brought together and framed by the poetry of Maj Ragain.

This strategy has several significant consequences: First, by preserving the integrity of the oral history archive and allowing mutually exclusive stories to be told, Hassler reminds us that for every plot or interpretation that is accepted by a listener because it appeals to preconceptions shared by a storyteller and his audience, there is another story that is viewed skeptically because key preconceptions—political, ideological, cultural or aesthetic—are not shared. In other words, the play shows us how historical "facts" can be changed through something as simple as a changed point of view.

A second important result of Hassler's method stems from the notion that being exposed to dissonant perspectives has clear benefits. Hearing what cannot be disconfirmed or negated is a potent antidote to the tendency we all have to become captive of our ideological or culturally constructed preconceptions. And since multiple interpretations are sanctioned, choosing one over the other is dangerous and problematic. Hassler implies that when a single truth proves elusive, a more mature type of wisdom is achieved through pluralism.

Finally, the response to tragedy endorsed in *May 4th Voices* is not one from inside the academy, but one derived from the voices of a community. This means

A Guardsman reading *The Plain Dealer* behind Wills Gym on May 4 at about 8:30 a.m. Photo by Chuck Ayers.

that in the play, the speaker of history and the audience are engaged in a meaning-making give and take that is more direct and perhaps purer than that found in traditionally "authored" accounts. If the historian is to be judged by the accuracy of his reproduction of external artifacts, then it would be difficult for anyone to argue that *May 4th Voices* is not both unassailably accurate and "true" in an unusual way.

At the end of our unit on *May 4th Voices,* I asked the class to draft personal responses to the play as a teaching tool in the literature classroom. One international student, an aspiring poet from Jordan, confided to me that she had initially known nothing at all about the Kent State tragedy. Her response nevertheless gave the best possible demonstration of why David Hassler's play is worth studying and why it moves audiences: *"Not teaching students about May fourth is like cheating them, simply because our history is part of our identity."*

## STUDENT RESPONSES TO MAY 4TH VOICES

*May 4th Voices* moved me more than any memoir or history text. The emotion of a memory being shared maybe for the first time is something that can't be duplicated, but the author took those thoughts and ordered them into a single whole. Reading this collection of voices gave me perspectives I had never heard previously. It felt like listening to a neighbor or relative, and it made the tragedy of Kent State feel less like the distant past and more like recent history.
—*Brittany Gregg*

The Vietnam War is not adequately covered as historical subject matter in schools. This play gave an honest account and focused on the truth. It gave a deeper insight than any textbook ever could. It was understandable and relatable. I am glad I learned about the Kent State shootings the *May 4th Voices* play. If I had read about it in a textbook I wouldn't have felt a connection. Certain stories in the play would never have been presented in a textbook, like the story of the student whose father died in the hospital and the stories of the national guardsmen. These stories are the essence of May 4th.
—*Sarah Oser*

After reading the *May 4th Voices* play, I felt a much deeper appreciation and understanding of the events that transpired. The biographical voices that run through the play have a definite sense of fear and hope, confusion and sadness. This work of art truly captivates the reader to not only understand all who took part in the May 4th events, but to learn how to apply this tragic moment to better our futures. This play is beautifully done and has the gift to transcend, to reach all levels and groups of people. It is the voice of truth.
—*Kristen Snyder*

For me, David Hassler's *May 4th Voices* play offered a comprehensive re-enactment of the emotions and tensions surrounding the Kent State shootings. Hassler has seamlessly assembled a cohesive narrative from the interviews with real people; the result is a work that not only communicates facts and dates, but depicts the emotional landscape of a community at the boiling point of social change.
—*Lauren Rossi*

The play was educational because it gave points of view from not only one side. It read almost like a testimony, but it worked effectively as a text when it got the soldiers' and students' perspectives, as well as the perspective of family members. Students should read this play because, as a student myself, it gave me a well-rounded view of the chaos of May 4th without sounding like a textbook.
—*Crystal Umberger*

The *May 4th Voices* play allowed me to become more aware of the Kent State shootings. It was very interesting to hear all the different accounts from the day and watching the production allowed me to have more insight. Students should read this play because it enables them to be more conscious of the fact that there was more than one side to the story. It is important to get all of the different perspectives so that students are able to form more well-rounded educated opinions.
—*Chelsay Jackson*

Reading the *Voices* play in class showed me that it can be read by anybody anywhere. Every student, regardless of background, can relate to this text because many of the speakers are their age. It is a valuable piece of literature that has incalculable historical meaning. It would also be perfect for a beginning drama class because it is so readable and relatable. The incident at Kent State needs to re-membered by everyone, but by students most of all.

—*Liz Ahlman*

This play presents a unique opportunity for any student interested in both May 4th and the cultural turmoil and conflicts of the era. Bound up with interesting sympathetic voices from all sides, *May 4th Voices* effectively portrays a significant moment in time.

—*Ryan Mohr*

This is an amazing piece that should be used in the classroom to raise awareness of this tragic event. David Hassler is a very talented man and has created the ultimate tribute to the survivors and victims of the Kent State shootings. The *May 4th Voices* play was intriguing; I really felt connected to each voice. It is not only a historic piece of literature, but a per-sonal story of the people who survived the event. I loved this play for its amazing message and I learned a lot about the era surrounding the Kent State shoot-ings and the event itself.

—*Katelin Dillon*

*May 4th Voices* is an incredible collection of multiple viewpoints that all converge on one important point: the events at Kent State had an impact on an entire community and affected more than just students and guardsmen. This is an emotionally charged, infor-mative play, and the collaboration of voices covers the story from every possible angle. It is a play that can be used to understand and analyze the shootings by gathering information from multiple sources. It is a great piece of literature that memorializes the event. Well worth reading and studying.

—*Joel Cavanagh*

Particularly with help and input from the author, the *May 4th Voices* play offers students an original work composed of real testimony. The play maintains a journalistic feel while also being aesthetically pleas-ing. Searching for the context of the voices contrib-utes greatly to an understanding of the events and the reactions of real people to them.

—*Tim Sturm*

The *May 4th Voices* Play features unique and honest perspectives from the many sides and positions on May 4th. David Hassler has synthesized a myriad of personal accounts of the May 4 events in an engag-ing, interesting, and moving way to form a work that emphasizes the individual experiences that were central to the events at KSU in 1970.

—*Taylor Harland*

Remains of the burned ROTC building at or about 9:00 a.m. on May 4. Photo by Chuck Ayers.

# IMAGE THEATRE: CONNECTION, COMPASSION, EMPATHY

*Katherine Burke, Director,* May 4th Voices

*Katherine Burke has directed two different productions of* May 4th Voices *by David Hassler: once for its premier in 2010 at Kent State University and again in 2012 for performances at the Oral History Association conference in Cleveland, Ohio, and for a subsequent videotaping. See page 18 for ideas about how to use the video of* May 4th Voices *in the classroom.*

Ma*y 4th Voices* was staged as the culminating event of a Devising Theatre course at Kent State University in the spring of 2010. The class of 13 students and one instructor was tasked with devising a performance in commemoration of the 40th anniversary of the events of May 4, 1970. A few of the students took the course because they were interested in May 4th issues, and already felt a connection to the victims of the shooting and a responsibility for honoring them. Most of the students, however, merely took the class because they needed a few more credits. In fact, most 21st-century Kent State students report that they feel very little connection to an event that happened decades before they were born (Garcia Cano).

This left us in a quandary. The performance of *May 4th Voices* was to be performed in front of an audience of 500 people, many of whom were witnesses to the shooting, some of whose voices were even featured in our script. How could we create a performance that would adequately honor them if the students did not truly care about May 4th? We needed to find a path to empathy, a way to connect ourselves to 1970.

We spent the first part of the semester learning about May 4 in the Kent State archives. We invited witnesses to speak to the class, and toured the historic sites on campus. The students researched Vietnam and the culture of the 1960s, all of which gave us a solid intellectual understanding of the events, but did not address the impassioned content of the oral histories in the play. How could college students

in 2010 establish a visceral connection to their 1970 counterparts?

We found our answer in Augusto Boal's Image Theatre techniques. Boal (1931–2009) was an activist, theatre artist, and politician from Brazil, whose Theatre of the Oppressed techniques are used worldwide to identify and overcome oppression. Image Theatre, one of the foundations of his methods, is the creation of sculptures, using only our bodies as the "clay," in order to distill and expand upon an idea. Image Theatre encourages us to think with our whole bodies, to move beyond words, to crystallize meanings, to place ourselves in other people's shoes. Boal began to experiment with Image Theatre as a way for people to quickly and fully explain what they meant without the encumbrance of words:

> When . . . I understood that most of the time we were using the same words to mean very different things, or different words to mean the same thing, but that never were those things, or feelings, or memories, completely rendered by the words, I started asking my students to make images. Make an image of family, an image of your boss . . . your memories, your desires, your country . . . make images. Of course those images don't replace words but they cannot be translated into words either— they are a language in themselves (Boal 174).

The process of creating imagery often has a dynamic, liberating effect on actors. It is a simultaneously simple and challenging exercise that asks people to communicate without language (most Image Theatre exercises are done silently). Anyone can do it regardless of age, physical ability, language, or previous experience. Michael Rohd, Artistic Director of Sojourn Theatre Company in Portland, Oregon, advocates the use of "sculpting" as a technique in applied and interactive theatre:

Sculpting is my favorite technique. There's not been a session I've done where it couldn't be used in some way. It's fun. It's intense. It's revealing. It asks human beings to communicate in a way that is not common but is not foreign either. It bridges language and cultural barriers and sets up possibilities that can lead to all sorts of other activities . . . It is always new and always powerful (65).

The Devising Theatre students began exploring with Image Theatre and sculpting on the very first day of class. We sculpted in every class session, as warm-ups, to explore ideas, to connect with each other, to "get out of our heads." One student, Sarah Coon, wrote about her experience:

. . . we start sculpting each other into pictures, and we're communicating. And it's effective. Really effective. I don't try to describe how I want you to look and we banter back and forth with "a little to the left, not too high, etc.," I come up to you, look you in the eyes to make sure you're okay with what I'm about to do, and I move you. The amount of trust in that moment alone is amazing, and that touch seems to spread through the group until we have this sensory language of our own that just grew organically. So we start forming these images; some are iconic, even reminiscent of some of our photographic research, some are more abstract, and you can feel how the group is responding to each. And it starts to build, each image serving as the catalyst for another.

## HOW TO USE IMAGE THEATRE IN THREE EASY STEPS

Our process began with simple games and exercises to help us find greater freedom and comfort in the process of creating images. All of these exercises (and hundreds more) can be found in Augusto Boal's *Games for Actors and Non-Actors,* an essential book for anyone interested in using theatre for social change and civic dialogue.

### Complete the Image (Boal 39–40)

The group separates into pairs. Each pair chooses one person to be "A," one to be "B." This game is non-verbal. The partners begin by facing each other and shaking hands, then freezing in mid-handshake. "A" removes herself from the image, while "B" stays completely still, holding his half of the image. "A" briefly examines "B's" image, and then re-inserts herself into the image in a new way. Perhaps she grabs "B's" arm from the side, perhaps she leans against "B's" back, perhaps she turns away and makes a face—anything is possible, so long as it creates a new image. "A" freezes in place. Then "B" breaks his pose and removes himself from the image, briefly examining "A." He returns to the image in a new way. The images may form familiar pictures (a confrontation, a truce, a family, a sporting event) or they may be entirely abstract, or they may alternate back and forth.

Complete the Image is an excellent exercise for teaching one's mind and body the process of creating images. It gives permission to do and be anything, with no judgment about whether an image is aesthetically pleasing, foolish, or potent. Images are just images.

### Pair Sculpting (Boal 181)

Pair Sculpting is an introduction to creating thematic images. Here, one person sculpts another into any image, inspired by a word, idea, or motif. If, for example, we were sculpting on the theme of "Emotions," one might sculpt his partner into an image that expresses "love," "fear," "joy," or any other such word. In order to become comfortable with the technique, first use familiar words and themes: sports, things/people found in school, occupations, etc.; gradually move toward more complex and abstract themes. Sculpting can be done in three basic ways:

1. After securing permission to use physical touch, the sculptor may manipulate her partner—body, arms, legs, hands, even face—as if it were clay. This is often the most potent form of sculpting.

2. If the partners do not want to use physical touch, the sculptor can instead manipulate his partner as if he were a puppeteer, pulling invisible strings to move his partner's limbs. Partners can also imagine a field of energy—like a cushion—around their bodies; one can move the other's arm merely by pushing and pulling on that invisible energy field.

3. One can also sculpt her partner by modeling what she wants her partner to do, so that her partner can create a mirror image with her body and face.

Any combination of these sculpting techniques can be used at any and all times.

Using Pair Sculpting, we began to create images of students, National Guardsmen, faculty, war, peace, protest, the draft, and more. We "dynamized" (Boal 177) the images, adding movement, shifting the images forwards and backwards in time and space. We created images with relationships to one another (e.g. a protestor and a Guardsman, war and peace, a teacher and student) and analyzed what we saw in each other's images.

### Circle Sculpting (Rohd 63)

The group stands in a circle with three people in the center. One at a time (and in no particular order), individuals may sculpt the group in the center in the manner described above. Anyone may enter the circle to sculpt the group in the middle. If a sculptor needs more people, she can pull them in from the circle. She can use specific people for their genders or physical characteristics. If someone in the sculpture no longer wants to be the "clay," he can say, "sub," and another person will come in and replace him.

Anyone may suggest a topic for sculpting. Often it is useful to begin with sculpting images of ourselves, and then to move on to images of May 4, or whatever topic you are dealing with (I have frequently used these techniques to address bullying in schools, for example). You can use headlines from newspapers, photographs, quotations, or any other current or historical source as inspiration for sculpting.

Through this exercise we could begin to examine multifaceted issues, complexities, and perspectives. In one particularly potent session, we were examining the relationship between the National Guardsmen and the students. The class sculpted an image of Kent State Students in 1970, sitting on Blanket Hill, lounging, enjoying the day. The sculptor then removed one person from the image and stood him up, facing the group, and posed him as if he were holding a rifle, making him into the image of a National Guardsman. In that moment, the students had a powerful revelation: May 4, 1970 was not an intentional battle between the Guardsmen and the students, but that the men in uniform were from, and part of, the community of young people that they were tasked with subduing. This image gener-

ated a lengthy dialogue about the fear young men felt when their numbers came up in the draft, avoiding the draft by enlisting in the National Guard, and the injustice of war.

## IMAGE THEATRE IN PERFORMANCE

The "verbatim theatre" script of *May 4th Voices* calls for non-realistic staging that can deftly shift from one location to another, one time to another, one character to another. It was in our blocking rehearsals that Image Theatre became a useful and powerful tool for creating compelling stage pictures and movement. Groups of students collaborated to create static or kinetic images that expressed the central meanings of scenes and moments. We experimented with images, utilizing ones that we found apt, discarding ones that were cumbersome or superfluous. Movement and imagery was used only when it supported the text; we wanted the voices to be foremost in our performance, supported by imagery only when necessary.

Several significant and expressive images came out of Image Theatre work from our class. One occurred in the monologue of a young teacher talking about a student being bullied:

> . . . I moved closer to Paul and stood next to him. And they started to pick up these little tiny gravel stones and bounce them, one by one, off Paul's chest. They weren't throwing them hard, but just tossing them—ping, ping. And slowly moving closer. There were maybe ten of them, and these were some big boys, many of them played football and were good kids. I mean they weren't, otherwise, violent kids. But you could see the rage coming over them . . .

In a kinetic image, the actor reading the voice of the teacher stood still, downstage center, while a mass of others crept, monster-like, behind her. They began to overpower her small frame, creating a menacing image of threat and oppression that provided a compelling visual metaphor for the feeling of impending disaster conveyed in the testimony.

The bullying image emerged seamlessly from the image preceding it, the image that broke things wide open for our class, the image that finally, physically, emotionally, viscerally bridged us to the people of 1970. In this image, the actors were tangled in a mass, struggling against each other, reaching their arms past each other, straining to grasp something or break through a barrier. The image was developed in class in Circle Sculpting, weeks prior to staging the scene itself, merely as an exploration of the themes of struggle and protest. We had no notion when it was created that it would organically re-emerge in staging the performance. Student actor Sarah Coon, who was instrumental in sculpting this image, reported that this was the breakthrough moment in our class, in which we found what we had been looking for all semester. Creating and being in the image made the students tap into a deep well-spring of empathy, not only for the people of *May 4th Voices,* but for all who live under and struggle against oppression:

Out of all this sculpting and shifting and moving and touching, we start forming this image of this

line with people straining to get through. They're reaching over and around and underneath with outstretched hands and fists, and for a heartbeat it's like the room stops. Because you can feel the entire group go, "That's it. We've all been trying to get there and this is it." Because you can use as many words as you want to describe this moment we're illustrating—fear, anger, oppression—but it's not the same as seeing it. And it just appears like magic in front of us. And you can almost feel it in your own body; that reaching out, that straining. No matter what the words or situation, you know that feeling. It's May 4th, it's the Berlin Wall, it's Stonewall, all at once. That image did in one nanosecond what it takes some art hours to achieve: true empathy.

Boal, Augusto. *Games for Actors and Non-Actors.* New York: Routledge, 1992. Print.

Garcia Cano, Regina. "A Moment Kent State Won't Forget." *New York Times* 4 May 2010: A20. Print.

Rohd, Michael. *Theatre for Community, Conflict & Dialogue.* Portsmouth: Heinemann, 1998. Print.

Students begin to gather on the Commons at noon on May 4. Photo by Chuck Ayers.

# USING KENT STATE UNIVERSITY LIBRARIES AND SPECIAL COLLECTIONS ARCHIVES

*Stephen Paschen, Kent State University Archivist*

*Students working on individual and group research projects will find easy online access to the rich resources of Kent State University Archives. This article explains the many resources available to students and how to access them. Ideas for engaging individual and group projects and activities are outlined on pages 20 and 21.*

Kent State University Libraries department of Special Collections and Archives, like other primary source repositories, provides a connection between raw historical data and interpretation of history in secondary sources like books and articles (both print and online), broadcast documentaries, and student projects. The department has three functions: collection of records pertaining to Kent State University history; permanent preservation of the records; and provision of access to these records by students and researchers of all ages. This brief guide, specifically written for teachers, provides information about how to access the May 4 Collection housed in KSU Special Collections and Archives.

The May 4 Collection is in fact a "collection of collections" comprised of over a hundred separate collections (from separate donors). Like other archived primary source collections, materials are not all available online. However, an ever-growing proportion of records (particularly photographs) are online and teachers may effectively use the May 4 Collection in their classrooms. The gateway for use of the May 4 Collection is the departmental web page: http://www.library.kent.edu/specialcollections/may4.

It is recommended that teachers review the components of the web page to assess how their students may use May 4 materials as part of a lesson plan. The menu items (on the left side of the web page) include the following ways of exploring the history of these events:

- **May 4 Collection Contents**—each collection is described briefly and a link to the finding aid is provided. A finding aid is a descriptive inventory that will help students find materials of interest. The materials themselves are most often not online, but are available to any student who corresponds via email with the department. Instructions for communicating with the department can be found on the web page by clicking on the gold "Ask Us" button on the far left of the page.
- **May 4 Collection Index**—allows researchers to see collections grouped by topic, type (such as photographs or audio recordings), or by name.
- **May 4 FAQs**—answers the most frequently asked questions about the May 4 shootings and their aftermath.
- **Bibliographies**—provides links to other May 4–related web sites, books, and articles.
- **Exhibits / Chronologies**—the chronologies provide the sequence of events.
- **Oral History Project**—personal accounts of the May 4, 1970, shootings and their aftermath. This site provides both the audio and textual transcript of over 100 oral histories.
- **History Day Help**—includes materials for producing a History Day Project.

## THE LIBGUIDE AND THE ORAL HISTORY PROJECT

Two of the most effective online May 4 collections for use in the classroom include the Kent Shootings Photographs libguide and the Kent State Shootings Oral History Project, both of which can be accessed easily from the May 4 web page.

The Kent State Shootings Photographs libguide page is the best way to locate online images. Available at: http://libguides.library.kent.edu/May4Photographs, this guide includes links to hundreds of digital photographs within the May 4 Collection.

Classroom lessons relating to the importance of copyright and proper citation may be appropriate for upper level classes. Photographs can be used with other sources (such as oral histories) to introduce students to the concept of using different types of historical sources to interpret and describe an event from the past. An interesting comparative project might include students examining photographs taken on May 4 and comparing the perceptions of what they see in a photograph to what they hear and read in the accounts of eyewitnesses found in the oral histories.

The Kent State Shootings Oral Histories page, http://www.library.kent.edu/oralhistory, provides an opportunity to listen to and read the accounts of eyewitnesses to the event. This part of the collection, comprised of over 100 interviews, may be searched in three ways: by Subject (like bayonets, peace movements, or student strikes), by Narrators' Roles (such as student, faculty, or guardsmen), and by the names of Narrators (those interviewed).

First teargas canisters are fired at 12:10 p.m. on May 4. Photo by Chuck Ayers.

# OTHER RESOURCES: USING THE VIDEO IN THE CLASSROOM

The video of a performance of the play *May 4th Voices* that accompanies this Teacher's Resource was created in the fall of 2012 at Kent State University using student actors. The experience for the actors, most of whom had only a cursory knowledge of the events of May 4th, 1970, in Kent, was profound. They came away from their work with a deep understanding of the people, culture, and social conflicts of the time.

In the words of one of the actors, "Last night we watched *Fire in the Heartland,* a documentary film about May 4th, which devastated us. After having spent these past few weeks immersed in the voices of the witnesses and victims of the shootings, we have begun to make visceral, emotional connections to the students of 1970. We questioned what our own purpose was, we talked about our own activism (or lack thereof), we marveled at how the very room we were sitting in—in the Music and Speech building—was one where students were locked in and held there by the police. We wept over the senseless deaths. We anguished over the thirteen seconds of gunfire. We are beginning to understand our responsibility to this piece."

The video can be used in a variety of ways in the classroom. You might have your students view it after an initial reading of the script and reflect on the different experiences of reading the script and viewing the performance. You might use it as a culminating activity after students have thoroughly read and discussed the play and rehearsed its scenes. Or, you may have students view the video scene-by-scene as you work through the play with them.

Note that the performance that was videotaped differs from the written version of the play in some ways. For example, some male voices are assigned to female actors. Historic photographs and video of Maj Ragain reading his own poem have been incorporated to add meaning and impact.

Discuss these differences with your students and have them reflect on how they change the meaning or emotional impact of the work as written in script form or performed for an audience. Also have them discuss how a few minimal props—a sheet that can be folded like a flag or twisted like the anguish experienced by so many that day—were used by the actors to enhance the portrayal of events and emotions that are part of the play's power.

To learn more about the process of creating a performance of this play from the actor's perspective, have your students read their blog at http://may4th voices.wordpress.com/

Encourage your students to blog about their own experiences with *May 4th Voices.*

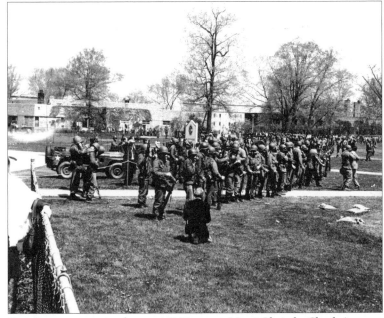
Guardsmen prepare to advance at 12:15 p.m. on May 4. Photo by Chuck Ayers.

# OTHER RESOURCES: MAY 4 VISITORS CENTER AT KENT STATE UNIVERSITY

Using images, artifacts and multimedia, the center's exhibits tell the story of the decade leading up to May 4, 1970, the events of that day, the aftermath and the historical impact.

Laura Davis, director of the May 4 Visitors Center and a Kent State freshman in 1970 who witnessed the shootings, said, "The May 4 Visitors Center offers a powerful and immersive experience that provides context and perspective on the tragedy, and examines the lasting impact that still resonates today." Davis added, "From the perspective of more than 40 years, the visitors center experience remembers the students who lost their lives on May 4—Allison Krause, Jeffrey Miller, Sandra Scheuer and William Schroeder—while offering meaning for today in their loss."

On Feb. 23, 2010, the National Register of Historic Places added the site of the May 4, 1970, shootings at Kent State to its official list of the nation's historic places worthy of preservation.

Visitors to Kent State can walk the steps of that history on the May 4 Walking Tour, which was dedicated on May 4, 2010, for the 40th commemoration. The tour features historic site trail markers and a documentary narrated by civil rights activist Julian Bond.

The May 4 Visitors Center is located in room 101 of Taylor Hall at 300 Midway Drive on the Kent State campus. The center is open from noon to 5 p.m. Monday through Thursday and Saturday. Admission is free. The center also will be open by appointment for group tours. Call 330-672-4660 or email may4@kent.edu for more information. For information on special events and seasonal changes in hours of operation, go to www.kent.edu/may4.

Guardsmen continue to advance; students now over hill top, May 4, 12:15–12:20 p.m. Photo by Chuck Ayers.

# INDIVIDUAL AND GROUP PROJECT IDEAS

**Field Experience**—Take a field trip to Kent State University's campus. Visit the memorial to those who died on May 4th and the May 4 Visitors Center. Write a reflective essay on the experience.

**Arts Connection**—Create photographs or drawings of the events that led up to and included the shootings of May 4th.

**Arts Connection**—Create a documentary using re-enactments or reconstructions of the May 4th shootings using historic photographs or by enacting and filming the events.

**Music Connection**—Research and create a Top 40 soundtrack for May 4th, 1970. Comment on any songs that may seem significant for the events of that day.

**History Connection**—Research the biographies of the four shooting victims at Kent State. Write a letter to one of them expressing the legacy they have left for those who seek social justice today. Explain how the world they left in 1970 has changed, for both the better and/or the worse.

**Theatre/Arts Connection**—Illustrate a costume drawing of one of the figures from *May 4th Voices:* a townsperson, a student, a faculty member, a National Guardsman, or an FBI agent posing as a hippie.

**Theater Connection**—Perform a monologue of 20 lines/sentences using one of the voices from one of the scenes. Monologues may be from one scene or pieced together from different scenes.

**Health/Psychology Connection,** *by Julie Healy*—Connect the play into a personal health unit with Maslow's Hierarchy of Needs. Discuss the basic physiological needs of life such as food, water, shelter, warmth and safety. What happens to higher order needs in life such as school work, relationships, and career when you fear for your safety?

**Communications Connection,** *by Julie Healy*—Compare communication problems between teenagers and parents to the issues of communication and intention surrounding May 4th. How do nonviolent protests turn violent? Was there a misunderstanding in communication?

**Mental Health/Ethics Connection,** *by Julie Healy*—Discuss how we respond to stress. Discuss moral and ethical decision making. How did differing views for and against the war push people past their presumed code of ethics into actions they would regret?

**Arts and History Connection,** *by Heidi Summerlin*—On May 4, 1970, the Ohio National Guard fired 67 rounds for 13 seconds at a group of students on the Kent State campus. At the end of the firing there were four students killed and 9 wounded. On that day, there were numerous photographs taken by student photographers due to the location of the shooting by Taylor Hall, the building that housed the School of Journalism. It is because of this that the events of the day are well documented. For this group project, organize into groups of three or four. Go to research websites and find photographs taken before, during, and after the shootings. Use these photographs to make your own chronology. Choose only 20 photographs. For each photograph you use, explain why you chose the photograph and how it fits into the order of events that occurred. Present your project to your audience using any of various media such as a Power Point presentation, book, or poster display using the photos.

# COMMON CORE CURRICULUM ACTIVITIES

## READING LITERATURE

*Grades 11–12, Standard 5: Analyze how an author's choices concerning how to structure specific parts of a text (e.g., the choice of where to begin or end a story, the choice to provide a comedic or tragic resolution) contribute to its overall structure and meaning as well as its aesthetic impact.*

Analyze the structure the author chose to use in communicating the events of May 4th, 1970. Analyze the aesthetic impact of the structure.

*Grades 11–12, Standard 7: Analyze multiple interpretations of a story, drama, or poem (e.g., recorded or live production of a play or recorded novel or poetry), evaluating how each version interprets the source text. (Include at least one play by Shakespeare and one play by an American dramatist.)*

Find two characters in the play that discuss the same specific topic. Compare and evaluate how each character interprets the "source text," i.e., a purely factual documentation of events.

## SPEAKING AND LISTENING

*Grades 11–12, Standard 1: Initiate and participate effectively in a range of collaborative discussions (one-on-one, in groups, and teacher-led) with diverse partners on grades 11–12 topics, texts, and issues, building on others' ideas and expressing their own clearly and persuasively.*

Read a common scene individually and then participate in discussions (one-on-one, small group, and teacher-led) building on others' ideas and expressing perspectives clearly and persuasively. For instance, discuss interpretations of what a certain character's words convey in a scene.

*Grades 11–12, Standard 2: Integrate multiple sources of information presented in diverse formats and media (e.g., visually, quantitatively, orally) in order to make informed decisions and solve problems, evaluating the credibility and accuracy of each source and noting any discrepancies among the data.*

Using news accounts (printed, radio, visual), interviews, poetry, etc. (Perfection Learning's collection on the Vietnam War, various news sources' reports, the Kent State Archives, etc.), integrate multiple sources of information presented in diverse formats evaluating the credibility and accuracy of each source and noting any discrepancies among the data.

## WRITING

Extended Response Writing Prompts noted in the scene-specific sections address these Common Core Writing Standards:

*Grades 11–12, Standard 1: Write arguments to support claims in an analysis of substantive topics or texts, using valid reasoning and relevant and sufficient evidence.*

*Grades 11–12, Standard 2: Write informative/explanatory texts to examine and convey complex ideas, concepts, and information clearly and accurately through the effective selection, organization, and analysis of content.*

*Grades 11–12, Standard 3: Write narratives to develop real or imagined experiences or events using effective technique, well-chosen details, and well-structured event sequences.*

*Grades 11–12, Standard 7: Conduct short as well as more sustained research projects to answer a question (including a self-generated question) or solve a problem; narrow or broaden the inquiry when appropriate; synthesize multiple sources on the subject, demonstrating understanding of the subject under investigation.*

*Grades 11–12, Standard 9: Draw evidence from literary or informational texts to support analysis, reflection, and research.*

# ADVICE FOR STUDENTS: COLLECTING AND WRITING ORAL HISTORIES

*Doris Baizley*

*Doris Baizley is a founding member of LA Theatre Works and worked at the Mark Taper Forum as resident playwright for the ITP Company for young audiences and dramaturg for the Other Voices Program for theatre artists with disabilities. Her plays* Mrs. California, Tears of Rage, A Christmas Carol, Guns, *and* Shiloh Rules *have been produced in U.S. regional theaters including A Contemporary Theatre, The Alabama Shakespeare Festival, Honolulu Theatre for Youth, Peoples' Light and Theatre Company, and The Mark Taper Forum. These suggestions are designed to help the playwright who is working with oral histories.*

As you work with the play, *May 4th Voices,* and investigate the Kent State University Archives, you will encounter the many oral histories that have been collected from people who experienced May 4th, 1970, firsthand. You can use these oral histories and the play as models for collecting stories from people who have experienced an important event and using them as a basis for your own creativity.

## FROM "SPIDER SPECULATIONS" BY JO CARSON, THEATRE COMMUNICATIONS GROUP, 2008

*Jo Carson (1946–2011) was an American playwright, poet, fiction writer, and actor, as well as the author of three children's books. Her best-known play is* Daytrips *(1991), and her poetry is collected in* Stories I Ain't Told Nobody Yet *(1989). Her story collection* The Last of the "Waltz Across Texas" *was published in 1993. Following are some suggestions about how to most effectively collect oral histories.*

**1. Story circles.** People from the community are invited to meet for coffee and story swapping around the specific subject. The value of the story circle is that one person's experience reminds others of their experience and the gleanings are usually rich. After the story-circle, storytellers are identified and paired with interviewers.

**2. One-on-one interviews.** Interviewers take a recorder, a note pad, and a release form that allows us to use the stories they gather. Interviewers use open-ended questions we've practiced beforehand. For instance, "Where are you from?" can be answered with two words: "Harlan, Kentucky." "Tell me about where you come from . . . " asks for a lot more and is more likely to get an involved response. "Who are your parents?" gets minimal response. "What are (or were) your parents like . . . ?" will always get more.

I try to get interviewers not to carry a set of questions to an interview. I'd rather they were comfortable enough with open-ended thinking that they don't have to. If people want a list, I ask them to make some open-ended questions before the interview. I don't provide the list because I want new interviewers to think of the questions they are going to carry with them.

I teach the interview itself as a fishing expedition: go for what you get, not what you thought you were looking for. Never go to an interview looking for "history." People will often not talk for fear of a faulty memory—or fear of not having an "important" enough story. Go on an interview to collect stories. Everybody has a story.

Learn to live with silence, without getting the fidgets or jumping ahead to the next question. It is active listening: how to encourage a storyteller without interrupting his/her thought. One memory usually calls up another and the trick is to wait for it graciously.

**3. Transcribing.** I transcribe the stories word for word, and work with the transcriptions using every trick I can think of to make the narrative interesting onstage. My job is to make something of what comes to me in the story, to find a theme, to make it coherent in some way, to make it simple, and powerful in performance, to take an audience on a journey with each piece as a whole. I play with ways narrative can be made dramatic without complete scenes.

## MAKING THE PIECE FOR PERFORMANCE BY DORIS BAIZLEY

**1. Recording Oral Histories.** Taking notes while recording often helps fill in the quiet moments, giving the storyteller some time to reflect. It also helps as a guide to the transcript later, and gives the storyteller a sense that what he/she is saying is important.

**2. The narrative/dramatic tricks.** Use the first person voice. Listen for speech patterns, language usage specific to your storyteller, repeated phrases, or terms of familiarity, and use them. They can help create rhythm or character or just fill in a transition to another part of the story.

The danger here is pushing the voice into caricature or mimicry, so read it to yourself out loud. Do this a lot. Don't act it, just read it. If it feels like you're making fun of somebody, cut back on the "color." If it feels like a story that could be told by anybody, find more. You don't have to make stuff up. When in doubt, go back to the transcript. Everything is there. Play with it.

Is there another character mentioned in the interview whose voice might come into the story? Sometimes it's stronger just to quote that character in your storyteller's voice, but there are times when another character might appear in person to punctuate, add to, or push the story beyond narration into bits of dialogue that create conflict or context.

Look for real material that might be mentioned incidentally in your teller's story (a rulebook, map, recipe, song lyrics, etc.). Real stuff can be useful for getting more information from your storyteller in the second interview. Or, it can be used by another voice in performance as a sort of real-world background to the story being told.

A desperate measure: use yourself if you have to. Sometimes your reaction to the storyteller can be the only way to start the story—or to finish it. (But remember, it's not about you.) The solution is probably in the transcript, or in your next interview.

**3. Structure.** Start transcribing after the first interview. As you discover a theme, an emotional through-line, or a feeling about where it's leading, or what it's saying, move stuff around. If you can't find a through-line, move stuff around anyway. Starting at a random spot may give you a new idea. Thinking of a title for the story can also be a way to trick yourself into finding a theme.

> **a. Chronology can be your friend:** Moving from "then" to "now" isn't a bad structure. And it can be a helpful way to organize your transcript.
>
> **b. Structure by Tone or Emotion:** Funny to serious . . . dream to reality . . . or, by content. What I thought then to what I think now . . . somebody else's experience to my experience. (And vice versa on all of these)
>
> **c. The Blow-Up Structure:** one small incident can be the frame for the whole piece—or it can be the whole piece. The second interview may be the time to find out more about the incident. Or maybe it's all in the first interview. (Don't worry. That happens a lot.)

# AN APPROACH TO ART PROJECTS
## RELATED TO *MAY 4TH VOICES*

*Noël Palomo-Lovinski, Associate Professor, School of Fashion Design and Merchandising, Kent State University*

*Students in Professor Palomo-Lovinski's class were challenged to reflect a personal point of view about the events of May 4th, 1970, in their work as designers. The approach described here can be modified to accommodate students working at a range of ability levels and in a variety of contexts. See the results of design projects by two of Professor Palomo-Lovinski's students on page 26.*

## PROJECT GOALS

For students to **articulate social issues** that concern them today in the context of May 4th at Kent State: the upheaval of governments in the Middle East, Occupy Wall Street, etc. Can we use art to show that history repeats itself?

For students to see the **connections between art and society**. What is art expressing? How does art capture the zeitgeist of the times? How does society use or respond to art as a way to express abstract concepts?

How to **use formal qualities of color, shape, line, composition, texture, etc.** to express emotion that helps a viewer understand the intended meaning of the artist. How can the artist interpret an abstract social concept and extrapolate meaning that can be conveyed in art?

## GOAL 1: ARTICULATION OF SOCIAL ISSUES

Students can do this as a group of 4 or 5 students and create a presentation that takes advantage of visual and oral communications. Students also may want to begin making notations in visual journals that can lend information to the formal art portion of the assignment.

Have students list and discuss what they already know about the issues and concerns surrounding the events of May 4th. Encourage them to analyze the play for over-arching themes and ideas and identify

emotions or feelings that are relevant to the series of events. Help them to understand the context of the political climate during this series of events.

Have students list and discuss events that are happening in their own time period. Ask questions such as these:

- How are Occupy Wall Street and the Tea Party movement alike and different? Why were people angry and how did they show opposition to government?
- How did cities respond to protestors? What was the mood of the country?
- What happened in the Middle East? What was the outcome of these protests and why did they occur?
- What are some other examples of social protest that has happened within their present context?

List other important historical instances of social protest: American Revolution, Tiananmen Square, Women's Rights, Civil Rights, Gay Rights, etc. Ask, What did they have in common with May 4th, and other instances of social protest? What were the emotional responses to any of these protests?

## GOAL 2: CONNECTING ART AND SOCIETY

Have students look at some of the following artwork:
- *The Death of Marat* by Jacques Louis David (1793)
- *The Third of May, 1808* by Francisco Goya (1814)
- *Liberty Leading the People* by Eugene Delacroix (1830)
- *The Uprising* by Diego Rivera (1931) (or any works by the muralists of the 1930s)
- *Guernica* by Pablo Picasso (1937)
- *Blast* by Adolph Gottlieb (1957)

Discuss the idea of zeitgeist, or "spirit of the times." What relationship does art have to a zeitgeist? What influence does any visual medium have on ideology or concept? Why does a visual medium connect with an audience quicker than other forms of communication?

Assign each artwork to a small group of students. Have students research and discuss the historical incidents that are the focus of the artwork. Discuss with students the formal attributes of the painting that indicate that the subject is about social protest.

Ask students what they think the artist was trying to do by painting the subject. What were the emotions that are expressed? How are formal qualities used as metaphor? What are the connections between a subject of a painting and an abstract concept? How does an artist express innocence, anger, frustration, change, hope, dedication, etc?

Have students find other examples of 2D or 3D work that expresses an emotion and uses metaphor (does not have to be political). Think in terms of periods of change in history and how that is reflected in artwork. (For more advanced students, encourage modern or contemporary art rather than traditional figurative work). Have the groups present their findings to the whole class. Encourage students to make research notations in their visual journals to help them with their final project.

literal and more conceptual. (Students may need to repeat this exercise a couple of times). The idea is that students should be making connections from literal subjects to a more abstracted expression of an idea. Students will also inadvertently or knowingly be communicating their own feelings, beliefs, or opinions towards the subject area. Encourage the student to take a point of view as this needs to be communicated though the artwork.

**Step 4:** Have the students create lists of formal attributes (color, texture, composition, line, etc.) that could be associated with their last list of words.

**Step 5:** Create a 2D or 3D artwork that utilizes those formal attributes. The students may want to create a series of preliminary sketches first to receive feedback.

**Step 6:** Have the student present the work and explain the work in terms of communicating the intended message. Encourage the rest of the students in class to comment on how well the student communicated their idea before and after their verbal presentation.

## GOAL 3: FINAL PROJECT AND PRESENTATION

**Step 1:** Have students choose an event dealing with social protest or social concern. Research the incidents that led to the event. Create visual research and put it into a collage for quick reference. Have students explain why the images are powerful or meaningful to them.

**Step 2:** Have students list words that describe these pictures. This can be very literal: big, dark, crowded, violent, etc.

**Step 3:** Have students use words that describe the words previously listed. This list should be slightly less

Guardsmen kneel and aim into Prentice Hall parking lot, May 4, 12:20 p.m. Photo by Chuck Ayers.

## Kiem Soát
### (Vietnamese for *control*)

"My inspiration for this Spring Evening-wear collection stemmed from the concept of two opposing forces fighting for control. I used leather, intersecting bodies to represent the National Guardsmen. I used silk chiffon and georgette to represent free-flowing, uncontrollable emotions that accompany youth. Throughout my collections, no matter how hard the leather tries to stifle and interrupt the chiffon, it always finds some way to break through. With gowns that interrupt themselves and fabrics that collide into one another, this collection is my own representation of the emotional turmoil that took place on May 4, 1970."

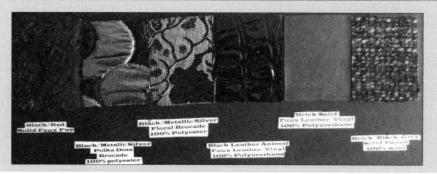

## May 4th

"One student in the play talked about how the pillars in Taylor Hall looked so strong and that they held up the whole building. But, when they were broken, she saw that they were only made of plaster and wire. This made her feel vulnerable to the world. In my collection, I took these emotions by creating very structured garments made from soft fabrics and wiring. These garments look strong and hard, but really, if you touch them, you see that they are only made of wire and fabric, like the pillars made of wire and plaster."

# COMMUNITY QUILT PROJECT

### ORGANIZING A QUILTING PROJECT

Community quilts comprised of squares each designed by an individual then sewn together, are an ideal way to commemorate an important event, tell the story of a shared experience, or provide a way for people to communicate with others through art and craft.

Participants are invited to tell stories using their own words, or words taken from oral histories. They may also create imagery using collage techniques to give visual form to ideas and emotions.

### MAKING A COMMUNITY QUILT

Have each participant choose a background square. In the quilt shown below, squares used for collage are 9-inch blue or black and squares for text are 9-inch white.

To assemble a collage square, back fabric pieces in various colors with heat set fusible web. Cut shapes from the collage fabric. Peel the paper backing from cut shape. Arrange shapes glue side down on blue or black background. Leave a ½-inch border. Iron the square to set the shapes in place.

For text squares, use Sharpie markers. Fill the square completely, leaving a ½-inch border.

The story quilt shown here was designed to patch together the community's memories of the May 4, 1970, shootings and to serve in healing a divided community. The quilt uses the symbolic colors of blue, yellow, white, and green: blue—peace; yellow—hopefulness, happiness, the sacred; white—purity; green—growth, renewal, strength. A local quilting group helped to put all of the pieces together and make the final product. This was a complete community project from start to finish. Photo by Anderson Turner. Courtesy KSU School of Art Galleries.

# ADVICE FOR STUDENTS:
# MAKING AN ORAL PRESENTATION

Making a formal presentation in front of a group of people can be frightening. Many people find the experience unnerving and try to avoid it if they can. But speaking, along with writing and listening, is an important way we communicate. Effective public speaking is perhaps one of the most important skills you can develop. Practice, and lots of it, is essential if you are to speak in public with confidence and communicate your ideas effectively.

Here are some tips that will help you write an excellent oral presentation.

1. Begin with a well-crafted introduction. It should include:
   - the type of presentation you will give: an informational report, an explanation of some thing, a persuasive argument, etc.
   - a statement of the thesis of your presentation and a preview of the main ideas you will cover.
   - an interesting story or fact that will grab your audience's attention.

2. Continue with the main body of your presentation.
   - Organize your main points in a logical order. If you're telling a story, use time order. If you're trying to persuade your audience, tell them how you want them to act and feel. If you are explaining a process, walk the audience through step-by-step.
   - Use concrete examples and illustrations for main points that are complicated or hard to understand.
   - Present information using graphic aids such as pictures, charts, and graphs.

   - Add details to make your presentation stronger. Anticipate questions your audience might ask and incorporate the answers into your talk.

3. End with a well-planned conclusion.
   - Summarize your thesis and main ideas to make sure your audience gets the big picture.
   - If appropriate, make a strong emotional appeal at the end of your talk.
   - Let your audience know what you want them to do as a result of your talk.
   - End on a positive note.

Here are some tips that will help you deliver your talk in a professional manner.

1. Know your audience. Be aware of how much your audience already knows about your topic. Make sure you are adding to their knowledge in an interesting way. Don't talk down to them or use terms and concepts they won't understand.

2. Rehearse over and over until you feel comfortable and can give your talk with confidence. Rehearse in front of others, before a mirror, and videotape your talk so you can critique it yourself.

3. Practice speaking slowly, with good enunciation and inflection in your voice, and with good sound projection.

4. Write each important point or idea on a separate 3" x 5" card. Number your cards in the order of presentation. Glance at them to keep your place, but don't read from them. Maintain good eye contact with your audience.

# EVALUATING STUDENTS' ORAL PRESENTATIONS

*To the teacher: Use the rating checklist on this page to critique oral presentations and suggest improvements. Suggest to students that they also use this form to evaluate each other as they rehearse. Use the Assessment Rubric on the next page to evaluate your students' final presentations.*

Name: _____

Date: _____

Class: _____

Topic: _____

Start time: _____ End time: _____ Duration: _____

Content

| | | | | | |
|---|---|---|---|---|---|
| introduction | 1 | 2 | 3 | 4 | 5 |
| clear thesis | 1 | 2 | 3 | 4 | 5 |
| logical order | 1 | 2 | 3 | 4 | 5 |
| use of visual aids | 1 | 2 | 3 | 4 | 5 |
| supporting information | 1 | 2 | 3 | 4 | 5 |
| conclusion | 1 | 2 | 3 | 4 | 5 |
| ability to answer questions | 1 | 2 | 3 | 4 | 5 |

Delivery

| | | | | | |
|---|---|---|---|---|---|
| confidence | 1 | 2 | 3 | 4 | 5 |
| enthusiasm | 1 | 2 | 3 | 4 | 5 |
| eye contact | 1 | 2 | 3 | 4 | 5 |
| appearance and posture | 1 | 2 | 3 | 4 | 5 |
| pronunciation | 1 | 2 | 3 | 4 | 5 |
| loudness | 1 | 2 | 3 | 4 | 5 |
| grammatical correctness | 1 | 2 | 3 | 4 | 5 |

Suggestions for improvement:

_____

_____

_____

# PROJECT ASSESSMENT RUBRIC

|  | 1 | 2 | 3 | 4 |  |
|---|---|---|---|---|---|
| **Organization** | Presentation lacks coherent organization. Audience is confused. | Student jumps around. Audience has some difficulty understanding the ideas presented. | Student uses a logical sequence which the audience can follow. | Student uses a logical sequence which adds interest and ease of understanding for the audience. |  |
| **Content Knowledge** | Student has only basic knowledge of the subject and cannot answer audience questions. | Student is unclear about some ideas and can answer only simple questions from the audience. | Student is comfortable with content and questions, but fails to elaborate on answers. | Student demonstrates excellent grasp of all aspects of the topic and answers questions completely with elaboration. |  |
| **Visual Aids and Supportive Handouts** | Student uses no visual aids or supportive handouts. | Student uses minimal visual aids or supportive handouts that provide little support for the presentation. | Student uses adequate visuals and handouts that support the presentation. | Student's visual aids and handouts explain and reinforce the presentation. |  |
| **Body Language** | Student reads from a script with little reinforcing eye contact or body language. | Student is uncomfortable and reads most of the report with little eye contact. | Student often refers to notes but maintains eye contact with the audience. | Student appears confident and maintains good audience eye contact throughout the presentation. |  |
| **Voice** | Audience is unable to hear the student because of poor vocal control. | Audience has difficulty understanding or hearing what the student is saying. | Student's voice is clear and pronunciation of terms is good. Audience does not have to struggle to hear. | Student uses a clear voice with correct, precise pronunciation. Good voice modulation and elocution adds to the presentation. |  |
|  |  |  |  |  |  |

# MAY 4TH VOICES BY DAVID HASSLER: OVERVIEW OF THE NINE SCENES

## Scene One: The Lottery
*Context: 1960s and the Vietnam War.* This scene provides context for scenes that follow. It begins with an introduction by Maj Ragain, a poet whose work explores his experiences during this tumultuous time period. Maj introduces the audience to Kent in 1969. The scene concludes with a tense confrontation between a high school anti-war demonstrator and other students. Voices of multiple characters are introduced (students, professors, National Guardsman, a professor, and a high school teacher).

## Scene Two: Something Drastic
*Thursday and Friday.* Tensions rise due to the warming weather and the threat of being drafted. Fires and vandalism occur in Downtown Kent and two elderly Kent residents are rocked inside their car.

## Scene Three: The Whole Town Is Burning
*Saturday and Sunday.* Townspeople and students recall Kent after the destruction of the previous night. National Guardsmen describe the orders they are given and a bloody confrontation with protestors is described.

## Scene Four: The Rally
*Monday Leading Up.* National Guardsman are "locked and loaded" on campus. Students begin to organize further protest. An African-American student expresses the particular concerns of members from Black United Students as campus tensions continue to rise.

## Scene Five: A Veil Is Rent
*The Shootings and Immediate Reaction.* The May 4th shootings are described. Students and National Guardsmen describe the events, both desperate and heroic, as the event unfolds.

## Scene Six: Intensive Care
*Later that Day.* The immediate aftermath of the shootings is revealed. Misleading newspaper head-lines are discussed. Students and a daughter, with a dying father in the same hospital as paralyzed shooting victim Dean Kahler, all relate their experiences.

## Scene Seven: Reactionary
*Throughout the Summer.* Townspeople connected to the University describe the hostilities directed towards them as a result of the shootings. The press attempts to manipulate a confrontation and a student attempts to make a citizen's arrest of Governor Rhodes.

## Scene Eight: Getting in the Way of Bullets
*Grand Jury & FBI Investigation.* The FBI get their man, who turns out to be a six-year-old boy. The fallout from the shootings results in questioning, ac-cusations of communist activity, thinly disguised FBI agents and 25 Grand Jury indictments, none of which include National Guardsmen or their superiors.

## Scene Nine: Vigil
*Legacy of Trauma.* Students and alumni reflect on the national significance of May 4th. They discuss the commemoration, recall the events, and explain the im-portance of May 4th in emotional, psychological, and spiritual terms. Poet Maj Ragain concludes the piece by exploring what May 4th means in today's world.

Jeff Miller in street, Dean Kahler on grass beyond street to right of Miller, May 4, 12:30–12:35 p.m. Photo by Chuck Ayers.

## SYNOPSIS

This scene provides context for scenes that follow. It begins with an introduction by Maj Ragain, a poet whose work explores his experiences during this tumultuous time period. Maj introduces the audience to Kent in 1969. The scene concludes with a tense confrontation between a high school anti-war demonstrator and other students. Voices of multiple characters are introduced (students, professors, National Guardsman, a professor, and a high school teacher).

## CONTEXT AND CONNECTIONS

**George Stanley McGovern**, born July 19, 1922, is an historian, author, and former U.S. Representative, U.S. Senator, and the Democratic Party nominee in the 1972 presidential election. McGovern's long-shot, grassroots-based 1972 presidential campaign found triumph in gaining the Democratic nomination, but left the party badly split ideologically.

**Draft Lottery** began on Dec. 1, 1969, when the Selective Service System of the United States conducted two lotteries to determine the order of call of military service in the Vietnam War for men born between 1944 and 1950. "The draft" occurred during a longer period of conscription in the United States from just before WWII to 1973. The days of the year were represented by the numbers 1 to 366 written on slips of paper. The slips were placed in separate plastic capsules that were mixed in a shoebox and then dumped into a deep glass jar. Capsules were drawn from the jar one at a time.

The first day number drawn was 257, on September 14, so all registrants with that birthday were assigned lottery number 1. All men of draft age, born 1944 to 1950, who shared a birthday would be called to serve at once. In fact the first 195 birthdates were later called to serve in order 1 to 195. The last date called was September 24, lottery number 195.

**Coxey's Army** was composed of unemployed workers from the United States, led by Ohio businessman Jacob Coxey, who marched on Washington D.C. in 1894, the second year of a four-year economic depression that was the worst in the United States to that time. Officially named the Army of the Commonweal in Christ, its nickname came from its leader and was more enduring. It was the first significant popular protest march on Washington and the expression "Enough food to feed Coxey's Army" originates from this march.

**The Moratorium to End the War in Vietnam** was formed as the war in Vietnam raged on and public opinion swayed against the war. On Oct. 15, 1969, an estimated two million activists from across the country gathered in Washington D.C. to protest the war. To this day, the Moratorium to End the War in Vietnam remains one of the largest demonstrations in American history.

**Vietnam Veterans Against the War** (VVAW) was originally created to oppose the Vietnam War. VVAW describes itself as a "national veterans' organization" that campaigns for peace, justice, and the rights of all United States military veterans." It publishes a twice-yearly newsletter, *The Veteran*, previously published more frequently as *First Casualty* (1971–1972) and then as *Winter Soldier* (1973–1975). VVAW considers itself as "anti-war," although not in the pacifistic sense.

Membership varied greatly from almost 25,000 veterans during the height of the war to fewer than a couple thousand in subsequent decades. While the member veterans were a small fraction of the millions that served between 1965–75, the VVAW is widely considered to be among the most influential anti-war organizations of that era.

**Students for a Democratic Society** was a student activist movement in the United States that was one of the main iconic representations of the country's New Left liberal political organizations. The organization developed and expanded rapidly in the mid-1960s before dissolving at its last convention in 1969. Participatory democracy, direct action, radicalism, student power, shoestring budgets, and its organizational structure are all present in varying degrees in current American student activist groups. Though various organizations have been formed in subsequent years as proposed national networks for left-wing student organizing, none has approached the scale of SDS, and most have lasted only a few years.

## INITIAL UNDERSTANDING

1. What were teach-ins?
2. What is napalm?
3. Who were the Students for a Democratic Society (SDS)?

## INTERPRETATION

1. What is ironic about the crowd's reaction?
2. Why would the SDS members face beatings and the singing of "The Star-Spangled Banner" by their assailants?
3. How have your own ideas about the events surrounding this scene changed as a result of reading this scene?

## REFLECTION

1. Why were 1967 and 1968 such stressful years in America?
2. What would a biology professor wearing a moustache suggest to his peers? Why were faculty members afraid of being considered "radicals"?
3. What concerns did Black and other minority students have during this time period? Why do you think they hesitated to join the Anti-War movement at Kent State?
4. Why do you think so many people showed up for the napalming of the dog?

## EXTENDED RESPONSE WRITING PROMPTS

1. Explain the assassinations of Martin Luther King, Jr. and Robert Kennedy and their impact on the U.S.
2. Respond to the following quote:

> I think the country came as close to a civil war between generations as you'd probably ever want to see. Because you had old versus young; you had fathers against sons; you had generation against generation. You can call it what you want. But Kent State brought to a boiling point the feelings on both sides.
> —Female Student 2

## SCENE SPECIFIC CROSS-CURRICULAR PROJECT CONNECTIONS

**Arts Connection**—Create a newspaper cover for the "Napalming the Dog" story.

**Literary/Historical Connection**—Using the Wordsworth quote about the French Revolution ("Bliss it was to be alive, but to be young was very heaven . . ."), relate the French Revolution to the Counter-Culture Revolution of the 1960s and 70s.

**Mathematics Connection**—Research the method Selective Service to choose draftees for the Vietnam War. What is your response to its design? Was the method fair or not?

**Literary Connection**—Research Maj Ragan and select one of his other literary works on the Vietnam Era. Can you find other thematic connections to *May 4th Voices*?

**Language Arts Connection**—Write a narrative from one of the following perspectives at the end of Scene 1: the high school anti-war demonstrator, the students whose brothers or fathers were fighting in the Vietnam War, or the high school teacher. Explore the thoughts and emotions that your individual perspective would be experiencing during this confrontation.

# SCENE TWO: SOMETHING DRASTIC

## Thursday and Friday

*David Massucci, Teacher of English, Theodore Roosevelt High School, Kent, Ohio*

### SYNOPSIS

As the early May temperatures rise, so does the tension across the United States. An escalation of the war by President Nixon intensifies opposition to it. Students and citizens in Kent are challenged by changes that they cannot yet define. For students, the draft continues to loom as an unwelcome possibility. For residents, the university setting becomes an obstacle to their daily tasks. In Kent, lives and conflicts begin to intersect as fire and vandalism occur downtown and a group of students harasses two elderly residents.

### CONTEXT AND CONNECTIONS

**Bombing of Cambodia** began in late April as the United States bombed targets in Cambodia, a country in southeastern Asia and a border nation of Vietnam. Described as an "incursion" by President Nixon, the bombing campaign sought to destroy or capture North Vietnamese weapons and equipment. Although it was successful in accomplishing some of those goals, the bombing of Cambodia also fed the Anti-War movement in the United States and was the catalyst for many demonstrations and protests.

**1-A Classification** meant that a man was qualified to serve in combat if drafted. Men who were between 18 and 26, and therefore of draft age, were classified according to their respective abilities to serve. The classification system also enabled men to seek postponement, deferment, or exemption from military service. For example, a college student could be granted a 1-S deferment for study. A 4-F classification meant that a man was physically unfit for service.

**Woodstock** took place over three days (August 15–18, 1969) on a farm in upstate New York. Woodstock was a music festival that became a legendary social and cultural phenomenon. Popular performers such as Janis Joplin, The Grateful Dead, and Jimi Hendrix attracted nearly 500,000 attendees, many of whom were united in their dismissal of authority and materialism and, by extension, the Vietnam War. Long hair, experimentation with drugs, and "free love" were hallmarks of the 1960s and Woodstock. These qualities symbolized a generational shift in priorities that was motivated in no small part by a desire for peace.

**ROTC** (Reserve Officer Training Corps) is a college program offered at many U.S. campuses. Students who enroll in ROTC programs receive training and tuition assistance while they are in college. In exchange, ROTC students commit to a period of military service upon completion of their studies. Campus ROTC buildings house these programs and serve as a contact and headquarters for ROTC students.

### INITIAL UNDERSTANDING

1. Where is Cambodia?
2. What is an RA counselor?
3. What is "cannon fodder"?

### INTERPRETATION

1. Male Student 1 has a "strange, cold feeling" as he walks past the ROTC building. What does this foreshadow? How is his feeling ironic?
2. Why would anti-war students view the ROTC building and/or ROTC students with suspicion or negativity?
3. Why is it significant that the couple in the car being rocked is an elderly couple?

### REFLECTION

1. How might having a 1-A classification influence students and their behavior?
2. How did gender influence the thought processes of students?

## EXTENDED RESPONSE WRITING PROMPTS

1. Would the Anti-War movement have been different if Woodstock had not happened? Explain.

2. For this assignment, create a conversation between the elderly couple in the car. The conversation should begin moments before their car is surrounded and conclude as they pull into their driveway, assuming they are on their way home.

## SCENE SPECIFIC CROSS-CURRICULAR PROJECT CONNECTIONS

**Historical Connection**—Research the rationale behind President Nixon's decision to invade Cambodia during the Vietnam War. Discuss the pros and cons of this controversial action.

**Musical Connection**—investigate the musical groups that performed at Woodstock. Choose one group that performed a protest song during the concert, analyze the lyrics of the song, and connect those lyrics to the time period and/or events of this scene.

**Journalism Connection**—Rewrite the events described in this scene as objectively as possible. Utilizing a journalistic approach, avoid any bias either for or against those involved.

A "strange, cold feeling" grips students as they pass the ROTC building. Photo by Mathias Peralta. Courtesy KSU Wick Poetry Center.

## SYNOPSIS

The intensifying emotions and violence of Friday night have carried over into Saturday and produced more destruction. The ROTC building has been burned to the ground, and the National Guard has arrived on campus in full force. Students provide their perceptions of a situation they do not completely understand and a town they cannot fully recognize. Members of the National Guard describe the still escalating tensions and recount various confrontations with students, citizens, and protestors. With no end to the conflict in sight, all sides struggle to find their paths to an increasingly elusive resolution.

## CONTEXT AND CONNECTIONS

**Governor Rhodes** (Sept. 13, 1909–March 4, 2001)—James A. Rhodes was governor of Ohio from 1963 to 1971 and again from 1975 to 1983. On May 2, 1970, in response to a request from Mayor Leroy Satrom, Governor Rhodes sent the Ohio National Guard to Kent State in an attempt to suppress the protests on campus. Although Rhodes was popular with Ohioans (he was elected governor four times), his reputation was damaged by the May 4 shootings and his role in them. In the years that followed, Rhodes was one of several defendants in a civil lawsuit filed by the victims and their families.

**Mayor Satrom** (Feb. 4, 1919–Sept. 8, 2004)—Leroy M. Satrom was mayor of Kent from 1970 to 1972. On May 1, 1970, Mayor Satrom declared a state of emergency in Kent. Concerned that his police force would be unable to prevent a dangerous situation from occurring, Mayor Satrom asked Governor Rhodes for help in the form of the Ohio National Guard. Mayor Satrom's tenure as mayor was brief, as he was elected Portage County engineer in 1972.

**Martial Law** is a form of military rule that can be instituted if the local government and/or police force are unable to maintain security and order. Martial law is temporary and can be enforced by state or national military forces.

**National Guard** is a reserve military force. The National Guard serves both state and federal governments. Although National Guardsmen can be called for combat service, they are often utilized in their home states during emergencies and following natural disasters. Members of the National Guard usually hold regular jobs, as the required training is limited to one weekend per month and a two-week period each year.

## INITIAL UNDERSTANDING

1. What is a Student Union?
2. What is an M1?
3. What does it mean to "lock and load"?

## INTERPRETATION

1. What do the City Bank's large pillars symbolize?
2. Why was it important to the captain for his men to march in cadence?
3. Why did the National Guardsmen remove their name tags from their jackets?
4. What is significant about Guardsman 1's statement that they "were there to preserve the peace"?

## REFLECTION

1. Male Student 2 mentions rumors involving a cache of weapons and snipers. How might such rumors have influenced the events in town?
2. What caused the contrasting reactions of the citizens to the National Guardsmen? In your response, consider the examples of the students

throwing rocks and the grey-haired lady offering cookies.

3. There are several manifestations of the "us versus them" mentality discussed in this scene. What are some of the examples? Why did this form of conflict—us versus them—seem to be so widespread?

## EXTENDED RESPONSE WRITING PROMPTS

1. Female Student 1 refers to Governor Rhodes' remarks being broadcast on the radio. Conduct some research to learn his exact statements and write them down. Then, as Female Student 1, write Governor Rhodes a letter responding to his comments.

2. Write a persuasive essay analyzing the response/presence of the National Guardsmen. Your analysis must be in paragraph form and contain a thesis statement. Provide details and examples from the scene as support.

## SCENE SPECIFIC CROSS-CURRICULAR PROJECT CONNECTIONS

**Geography Connection**—Create a topographical map of the Kent State Campus during the shootings.

**Speech/Rhetoric Connection**—Find a transcript of Governor Rhodes speech and identify what might have been considered inflammatory speech/rhetoric at the time.

Emotions intensify as the National Guard arrives on campus. Photo by Mathias Peralta. Courtesy KSU Wick Poetry Center.

# SCENE FOUR: THE RALLY

## Monday Leading Up

*Nikki Marchmon-Boykin, Teacher of History, Theodore Roosevelt High School, Kent, Ohio*

### SYNOPSIS

In Scene Four, two students give their perspective on the presence of the National Guard on the campus of Kent State University. They also provide their interpretation, based on personal experience, of the right to or cost of student activism as well as what the presence of the National Guard symbolized given the time period and climate of the country and campus.

### CONTEXT AND CONNECTIONS

**United States Invasion of Cambodia** was a military strategy to flush out Vietcong headquarters in order to win or take control over the situation in Cambodia. War had appeared to be winding down after increased public outcry (as a direct response to the My Lai Massacre) and invasion of Cambodia was in direct contrast to what the average American citizen wanted in relationship to United States involvement in the Vietnam War. Protests across the country as well as at Kent State University occur.

**First Amendment** (United States Constitution) provides for the freedom of speech and assembly.

**The Riot Act** is read to disperse people from downtown Kent bars after Kent Mayor Leroy Satrom declared a "state of emergency." The State of Emergency was reported to be in response to protests and general unrest (spontaneous anti-war protests, vandalism of downtown businesses, blocked traffic, aggressive behavior toward law enforcement, bonfire set) in downtown Kent. Origins of a "riot act" are from Great Britain, which gave authorities the right to declare the unlawful gathering of twelve or more people as unlawful and to assign punitive measures. The Riot Act was said to have been adopted by the United States in the late 1800s.

**Black United Students** was a Black student organization established on the campus of Kent State University in 1968 to address the concerns of Black students and demand the establishment of a Black Studies Program on campus.

**The Black Panther Party** was organized in 1967 in Oakland, California. Considered a militant organization, during the Civil Rights Movement, that illuminated the role of the police in black communities (police brutality and racial profiling) and called for self-defense of one's home and community. The Black Panther Party also organized cooperatives while providing services such as food, clothing, education and legal services to the black and poor communities in urban cities across the United States.

**Teamster Strike** took place in Akron, Ohio, and resulted in the National Guard being called in to protect residents and strikebreakers from Teamsters (union members) who were reportedly armed.

### INITIAL UNDERSTANDING

1. What is the significance of the following to the scene you have just read: The United States invasion of Cambodia, First Amendment, The Riot Act, Black United Students, The Black Panther Party, 1970 Teamster Strike (Akron, Ohio).
2. Read transcripts or listen to interviews of individual recollections of the May 4th shootings. Identify their perspectives regarding the following: presence of National Guard (student, KSU Administration, City of Kent community members), safety concerns, campus climate (political, social/racial).

### INTERPRETATION

1. How did the climate of the country and local events affect or precipitate the shootings at Kent State University?

2. How did personal experiences, education and race influence the perspectives of students in regards to the presence of the National Guard on the campus of Kent State University?

3. How were the reactions of students, campus officials, law enforcement/National Guard, and Kent residents influenced by differing perspectives on the war in Vietnam and the right to freedom of speech and peaceable assembly?

## REFLECTION

1. In scene four, Male Student 1 commented, "I can't believe somebody didn't have the anticipatory skills to read that one." Given the climate of the country and the most recent assignment of the National Guard dispatched to Kent State University, how could university officials have better anticipated student and National Guard reactions to one another possibly averting the shootings?

2. Why might have Male Student 2 found the moments prior to the shootings "surreal?"

## EXTENDED RESPONSE WRITING PROMPTS

1. In scene four, Male Student 1 challenges his Abnormal Psychology instructor for "[holding] class without referencing the fact that there was a National Guard member standing at our doorway holding an M-1." What obligation do educators have to address or discuss current, yet controversial, topics within their classrooms to help or allow students process "real world" scenarios within the context of class content?

2. Write a dialogue between a member of Black United Students and one of their parents regarding the presence of the National Guard on the campus of Kent State University. Considering the climate of the country and campus, what commentary, suggestions, and cautions might be offered between the two?

## SCENE SPECIFIC CROSS-CURRICULAR PROJECT CONNECTIONS

**Music Connection**—Analyze musical references to May 4th shootings and create a collage or other visual representation of the varying reactions to the shootings.

**Historical Connection**—Research, compare and contrast the climate (politically, socially and racially) on college campuses across Ohio.

Students gather at a rally to protest the presence of the National Guard. Photo by Mathias Peralta. Courtesy KSU Wick Poetry Center.

# SCENE FIVE: A VEIL IS RENT

## The Shootings and Immediate Reaction

*Nikki Marchmon-Boykin, Teacher of History, Theodore Roosevelt High School, Kent, Ohio*

In Scene Five, the May 4th shootings and the aftermath are described from the perspective of students and National Guardsmen. The chaos and confusion of the shootings are described from these multiple points of view. Students prepare to further confront the National Guard. Professor Glenn Frank is successful in calming the troubled students and working to make sure further confrontation does not develop. A student describes her journey that day back to Cleveland and the tearful reception she receives from her mother and concerned neighbors.

## CONTEXT AND CONNECTIONS

**"13 Seconds 67 Shots"** refers to the length of shooting time and the number of shots fired by the National Guard.

**Glenn Frank** was a Kent State University Geology Professor who stood between Kent State University students and National Guardsmen after the shooting, calling for calm and possibly averting subsequent shootings.

**Passover** is a Biblical reference. It is the commemoration of the emancipation of the Israelites from the Egyptians and slavery.

## INITIAL UNDERSTANDING

1. Explain the significance of the following to the scene you have just viewed: "13 Seconds and 67 Shots," Glenn Frank, Passover
2. Compare and contrast student responses to May 4th Shootings and National Guardsmen responses to May 4th Shootings.

## INTERPRETATION

1. Read transcripts or listen to oral recollections of the May 4th shootings. What factors may have influenced the differing responses to the shootings?

2. What is the difference between the perception and reality of the experience of gun violence?

## REFLECTION

1. Why had the 13 seconds of gun fire "felt like an eternity" to Male Student 1?
2. Respond to Female Student 1's commentary on the stopping of time as it relates to the violent death. Do you agree with her? Why or why not?
3. What may have accounted for the differing responses of students to the May 4th shootings and how do you think you would have responded?
4. What obligation do educators have to protect their students in dangerous situations? Explain your answer.

## EXTENDED RESPONSE WRITING PROMPTS

1. Write a letter from a student who survived the May 4th shootings to a student on a different college or university campus. Give your perspective on the importance of student activism in the wake of this tragedy. Would you recommend that students continue protesting or not? What are the realities of student activism? Is student activism worth the cost of lives?
2. Create a stream of consciousness narrative or reactionary monologue in the voice (and mind) of Professor Glenn Frank as he stood between the students and National Guardsmen.
3. Using the Twitter Social Media platform, create tweets that record the responses from a) students or b) National Guardsmen to the shootings and/or aftermath on May 4th.

## SCENE SPECIFIC CROSS-CURRICULAR PROJECT CONNECTION

**Historical Connection**—Research the Kent Professor, Glenn Frank. Write a letter to him expressing your feelings about his actions.

# SCENE SIX: INTENSIVE CARE

## Later that Day

*Christina Dreher-Rodesheim, Teacher of History, Theodore Roosevelt High School, Kent, Ohio*

## SYNOPSIS

In the immediate aftermath of the shootings communication is cut off, no telephone calls coming in or out of Kent. Newspaper headlines are confusing and no one really knows what to believe or what to do. Everyone is in a daze and cannot believe what has happened. Students are worried about parents and parents are worried about their children. Townspeople are scared and some citizens of Kent pack up and leave town. In the end, one student is torn between the senseless shootings and her father's death all on the same day.

## CONTEXT AND CONNECTIONS

**Pilgrimage** is a journey or search of moral or spiritual significance. Typically, it is a journey to a shrine or other location of importance to a person's beliefs and faith, although sometimes it can be a metaphorical journey in to someone's own beliefs.

**Radicals** are individuals who endorse political principles focused on altering social structures through revolutionary means and changing value systems in fundamental ways.

## INITIAL UNDERSTANDING

1. What was the reaction of each of the voices?
2. What did the newspaper headlines report?

## INTERPRETATION

1. Why were the telephone lines shut off?
2. Why was everything in Kent shut down and students sent home? (Kent City School students? Kent State students?)

3. Why did some citizens of Kent pack up their homes and leave town?
4. Why were the newspaper headlines misleading and inaccurate?

## REFLECTION

1. Explain the emotions in this scene. What are the voices feeling as they sort out the events of May 4th?

## EXTENDED RESPONSE WRITING PROMPTS

1. Imagine you are living in Kent on May 4th, 1970. What is your response to the events on campus. Explain your feelings, your reactions to the shootings.
2. Research headlines and newspaper reports from the days immediately after the shootings. Compare and contrast these primary documents to secondary documents on May 4th. When did people get a clear picture of what really happened that day?
3. Compare and contrast the aftermath of the May 4th tragedy to a current tragic event such as Sept. 11, 2001. How have governmental and media responses to these types of events changed? In this era of technology do we respond in similar ways? Explain.

## SCENE SPECIFIC CROSS-CURRICULAR PROJECT CONNECTION

**Music Connection**—Find a copy of Ray Stevens' "Everything Is Beautiful" and identify why the lyrics and tune seemed so dissonant to the speaker after the events of May 4th.

# SCENE SEVEN: REACTIONARY

## Throughout that Summer

*Christina Dreher-Rodesheim, Teacher of History, Theodore Roosevelt High School, Kent, Ohio*

### SYNOPSIS

In this scene the voices are learning to cope with everyday life in the aftermath of May 4th. Unfortunately, people do not come together to comfort one another. Neighbors, once friendly, pick sides and judge. It becomes a world of Kent State students and faculty verses community members. Families split even more on the anti-war verses pro-war question. Anyone associated with the University cannot escape the hate and those who witnessed that terrible day wonder if their lives will ever be the same.

### CONTEXT AND CONNECTIONS

**Communist** is an individual who endorses a revolutionary socialist movement to create a classless, moneyless and stateless social order structured upon common ownership of the means of production, as well as a social, political and economic ideology that aims at the establishment of this social order.

**Governor Rhodes** (Sept. 13, 1909–March 4, 2001)— James A. Rhodes was governor of Ohio from 1963 to 1971 and again from 1975 to 1983. On May 2, 1970, in response to a request from Mayor Satrom, Governor Rhodes sent the Ohio National Guard to Kent State in an attempt to suppress the protests on campus. Although Rhodes was popular with Ohioans (he was elected governor four times), his reputation was damaged by the May 4 shootings and his role in them. In the years that followed, Rhodes was one of several defendants in a civil lawsuit filed by the victims and their families.

**Citizen's arrest** is an arrest made by a person who is not acting as a sworn law-enforcement official.

**Criminal Misconduct** is a legal term meaning a wrongful, improper, or unlawful conduct motivated by premeditated or intentional purpose or by obstinate indifference to the consequences of one's acts.

**Felony** is as a crime punishable by death or imprisonment in excess of one year.

### INITIAL UNDERSTANDING

1. What happened to the children playing in the sandbox? How is this a reflection of what was happening in the U.S. in 1970?
2. Explain the tension between the Guardsman, faculty, and students?

### INTERPRETATION

1. Why did people choose sides?
2. Why did Male Student 1 go down to Columbus to arrest the Governor?
3. Why were students asked if they were communist?

### REFLECTION

1. Explain the conflict between Guardsman 1 and Faculty. What is Faculty's attitude toward the Guardsman? Would this happen today? Why or why not?

### EXTENDED RESPONSE WRITING PROMPTS

1. Put yourself in the shoes of a student and then in the shoes of a Guardsman; explain how you would react to the criticism each faced in the aftermath of May 4th. How do you think you would have handled the situation?
2. Explain the role of the media in the aftermath of the shootings. How did the media shape public opinion?

### SCENE SPECIFIC CROSS-CURRICULAR PROJECT CONNECTION

**Music Connection**—Find a recording of "The Cherubini Requiem." Listen to the recording and comment on why the piece would resonate with the witnesses of the events of May 4th.

## SYNOPSIS

FBI agents arrive at the Erwin home in Kent, Ohio, asking to interview Matthew Erwin, who turns out to be a six-year-old boy. Their intended person of interest is not Matthew but Michael Erwin, Matthew's eldest brother. Michael recalls how the agents seemed intent on finding a source to blame for the violence, and how their focus landed on him. It started with the agents questioning him that day but continued beyond that, from him being stopped by local police officers while driving to having insults shouted at him in the courthouse in front of the Grand Jury. This scene shows the fallout from the shootings resulting in questioning, accusations of communism, poorly disguised FBI agents and 25 Grand Jury indictments, none of which would include National Guardsmen or their superiors.

## CONTEXT AND CONNECTIONS

**FBI** (Federal Bureau of Investigation) is a government law enforcement agency whose focus is to "protect and defend the United States against terrorist and foreign intelligence threats, to uphold and enforce the criminal laws of the United States, and to provide leadership and criminal justice services to federal, state, municipal, and international agencies and partners."

**Grand Jury** is a group of jurors whose job it is to decide if someone should be charged with a crime.

**Attorney General** is the main legal advisor to the government in a specified jurisdiction.

**Jefferson Airplane** was an American psychedelic rock band of the 1960s and early 1970s.

## INITIAL UNDERSTANDING

1. What is a "hippie"?
2. What does it mean to be indicted?
3. What does it mean to exonerate?

## INTERPRETATION

1. Why would it matter who played at homecoming?
2. What does Male Student 2 mean when he says, "they were setting the stage for a whitewash" (37)?

## REFLECTION

1. What was the atmosphere in Kent during the days immediately following May 4th, 1970?
2. What is reasonable, or not, about the FBI agents' questioning of Michael Erwin?

## EXTENDED RESPONSE WRITING PROMPTS

1. Explain why, in the context of the setting, the agent at the courthouse commented on the appearance of Male Student 1.
2. Explain the scene at the Portage County Courthouse from the point of view of a Grand Jury member or courthouse employee.
3. Retell the opening events of this scene from the point of view of Matthew Erwin 10 or 20 years after the fact.

## SCENE SPECIFIC CROSS-CURRICULAR PROJECT CONNECTION

**Historical Connection**—Research the indictment of the Kent 25. What did this indictment say about the motives of those bringing the case to court?

# SCENE NINE: VIGIL

## Legacy of Trauma

*Margana Fahey, Teacher of English, Theodore Roosevelt High School, Kent, Ohio*

## SYNOPSIS

This scene provides the perspective of looking back—reflecting—on the events surrounding May 4th, 1970. Students and alumni reveal the emotional and psychological impact of being involved in or related to the events of that day. They discuss the tension felt in the days and weeks afterward and the anger that continued to mount as few to none talked openly about the causes and outcomes of the day's events. Alumni share how vivid the events of 1970 seem to them when they return to campus years later for commemoration ceremonies. They ponder how aware people are now of what happened at Kent State in the spring of 1970 and what their role may be in promoting healing. Maj Ragain concludes the piece by exploring May 4th's meaning today.

## CONTEXT AND CONNECTIONS

**Post-Traumatic Stress** (PTSD) is defined as "a mental health condition that's triggered by a terrifying event. Symptoms may include flashbacks, nightmares and severe anxiety, as well as uncontrollable thoughts about the event."

**"Kent 25"** is the name given to the 25 Kent State University students and faculty indicted by a grand jury for their involvement in events of May 4th, 1970.

**Jackson State** is the site of the deaths of two young men, resulting from shots fired by police amid campus unrest, on May 14th, 1970.

## INITIAL UNDERSTANDING

1. What does *viscera* mean?

## INTERPRETATION

1. What does Female Student 1 mean when she says, "This was not Pearl Harbor" (39)?

2. Why would a student say, "[Kent State] was like the ideal place for the government to make an example of the student protest and anti-war movement?"

3. What "sixties' values" (40) appear in this scene or throughout the play?

## REFLECTION

1. How would Post-Traumatic Stress affect an individual? How might it affect a community?

2. Forty years later, are you satisfied that "the truth has been told" (41)?

3. How is May 4th, 1970, at Kent State a symbol "for everything . . . of everything at that time" (40)?

## EXTENDED RESPONSE WRITING PROMPTS

1. How were the events at Kent State "different than Jackson State" (39) in the spring of 1970? How were they similar?

2. What memorials to the events of May 4th, 1970 exist at Kent State University (or elsewhere) today? Where are they and why?

3. What events in your community's history deserve to be commemorated?

4. How could you encourage future generations to know the past?

5. What can everyone, regardless of where or when they live, learn from what happened at Kent State on May 4, 1970?

## SCENE SPECIFIC CROSS-CURRICULAR PROJECT CONNECTION

**Historical Connection**—Research the events that occurred at Jackson State and compare and contrast them to events that occurred at Kent State.

**Medicine/Psychology Connection**—Research Post Traumatic Stress Disorder and how this diagnosis was identified and treated after the Vietnam War and today.

# A FINAL THOUGHT

*David Hassler, author of* May 4th Voices: Kent State, 1970

"When two people discover that parallel experiences led them to contrary conclusions, they are more likely to hold their differences respectfully, knowing that they have experienced similar forms of grief. The more you know about another person's story, the less possible it is to see that person as your enemy . . . When we share the sources of our pain with each other instead of hurling our convictions like rocks at 'enemies,' we have a chance to open our hearts and connect across some of our great divides."

—Parker J. Palmer, *Healing the Heart of Democracy*, 2011

I received the letter on the following page from a friend who graciously shared with me his reaction to a performance of the play I created, *May 4th Voices: Kent State, 1970.* I include it here because my friend's perspective on the events and circumstances surrounding May 4th, 1970, as he experienced them, are different from my own.

Dealing with controversy and conflict in a classroom setting is a challenge. Sharing and discussing this letter with your students will, I hope, offer an opportunity to model respect for personal experience and the diverse ideas, emotions, and conclusions individuals draw from those experiences.

David,

I was hoping to share my thoughts with you about your epic May 4th work. As someone who was as close to this event as most, I thought it critical that you hear a voice from the world of the students throwing pebbles. In reference to the scene of the play about the incident at Kent Roosevelt High School, I believe the individual was Paul, a Junior classmate of mine.

I think it's critical that the event is not taken out of context. To give you some clarity of context, remember some important issues:

- Most of the parents of the students at Kent and the older citizens of the town lived through WWII.
- Many fought in the war and saw their friends or family members spill their blood and make the ultimate sacrifice for our country on the beaches Normandy, Guadalcanal, Pelileu or Okinawa and many other battle fields so far away.
- Most of the town's people loved Kent State, as my parents did.
- They saw their school being "over taken" by radicals, i.e. the SDS, BUS occupying buildings, protesting the war.

My father, a 1943 graduate of Kent, whose grandfather, Frank Merrill, laid the cornerstone of the first building on campus (Merrill Hall) was a decorated Marine Corp Captain who fought in the South Pacific. He carried the symptoms of PTSD around his entire life as well as he could. He never talked about the atrocities of his time in battle. I believe that he saw his fellow Marines' graves, being trampled on by those radical students. Us kids heard about it every night at the dinner table.

So there was a mix in our town of young, "out of town radicals" and conservative town's people with strong ties to KSU. A toxic cocktail was brewing.

There was no doubt the National Guard should have been on campus, but armed with riot gear not M-16's. I think there was a rumor that there was a discovery of a van with a cache of weapons headed to OSU a few weeks prior to May 4th that may have been the impetus behind the Guard's weapons.

I tried to explain a viewpoint from someone who lived through May 4th. From my perspective, the representation in the play of the town's people was a bit harsh and I think it comes from a lack of applying the appropriate context for the times.

Thanks for reading, nice work.

Richard M. Foote